RESPONSIBILITY IS ...

by Michaela Castillo

Copyright © 2025 Michaela Castillo.
All rights reserved. No part of this publication may be reproduced, distributed, or transmitted in any form without the prior permission of the publisher.

ISBN: 9798308688532 (Paperback)

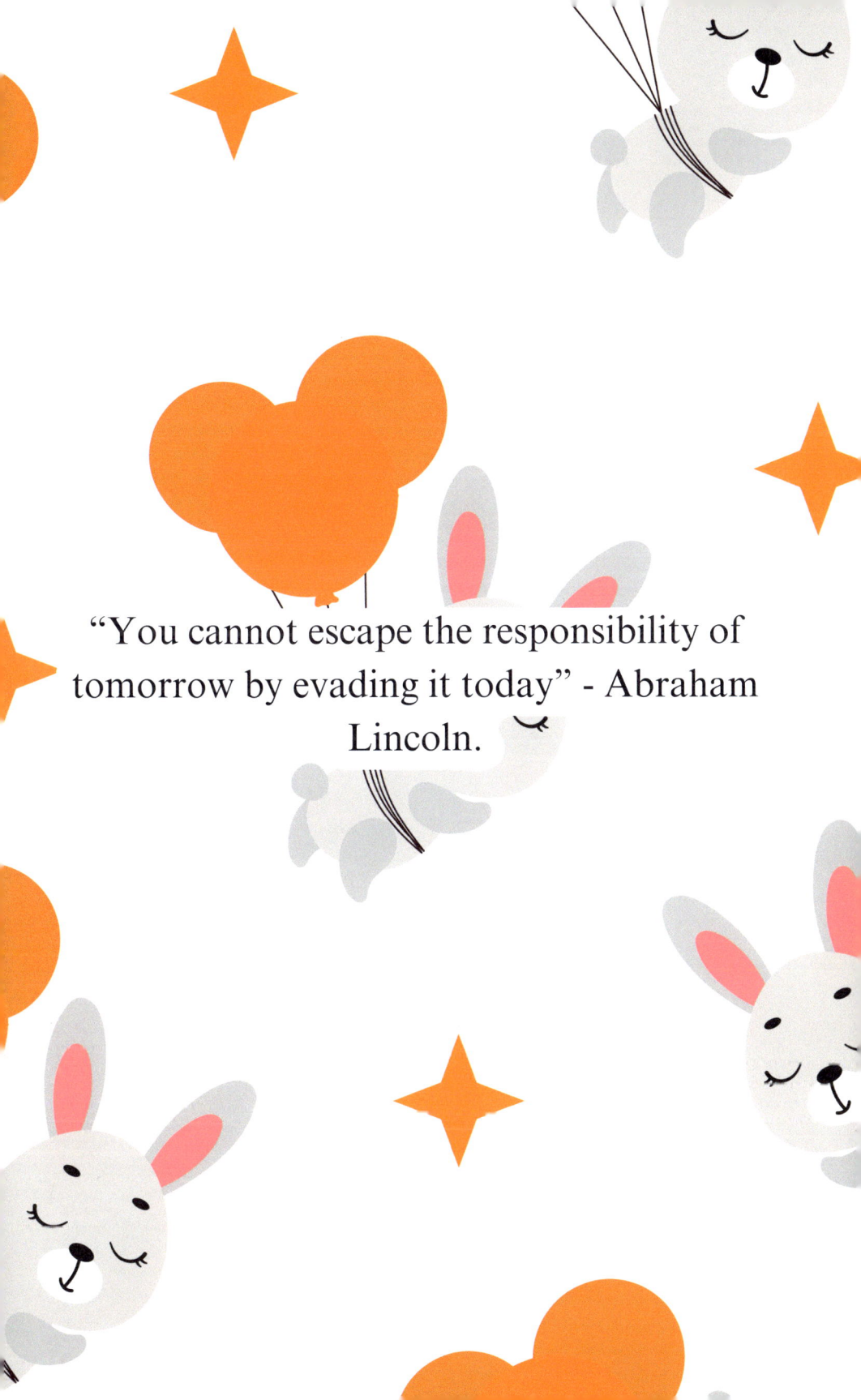

"You cannot escape the responsibility of tomorrow by evading it today" - Abraham Lincoln.

RESPONSIBILITY IS ...

by Michaela Castillo

Responsibility is...

Waking up on time

Brushing your teeth and making them shine.

It's placing your shoes in the right spot each day,

And finishing your homework before you go play.

It's feeding the pets and cleaning their space,

And keeping the yard a nice, tidy place.

It's picking up toys when you're done,

And saying "Please" and "Thank you," just for fun!

It's doing your chores, even when you're beat,

And giving your best in every task you complete.

Be Responsible

It's keeping promises, and staying true,

Doing your best in all that you do.

Responsibility helps you stand tall,

It's learning, growing, and giving your all.

So, one day you'll look back and see,

What a responsible person you've grown to be.

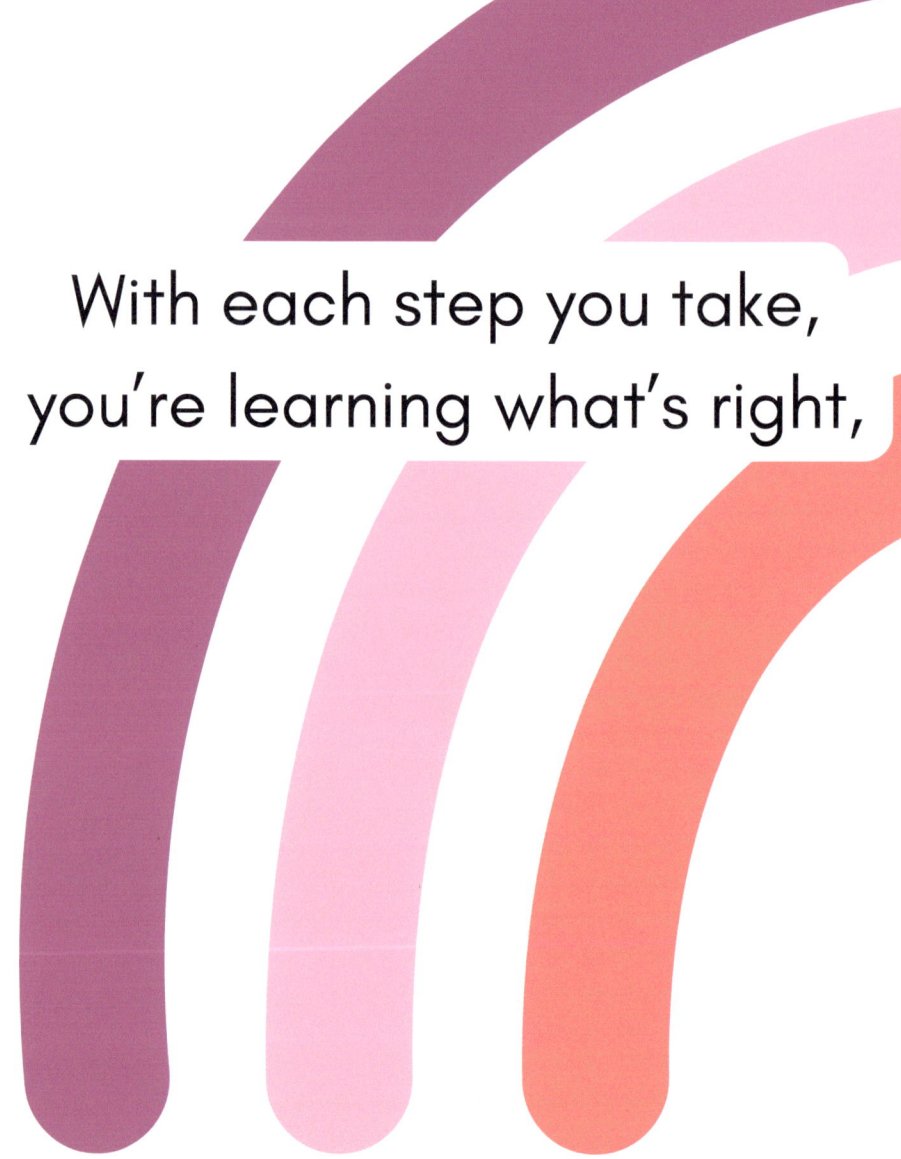

With each step you take,
you're learning what's right,

And that, my dear friend, is a beautiful sight.

Made in the USA
Columbia, SC
18 February 2025